Arts of a Cold Sun

Arts of a Cold Sun

Poems by G. E. Murray

University of Illinois Press

Urbana and Chicago

© 2003 by G. E. Murray
All rights reserved
Manufactured in the United States of America
1 2 3 4 5 C P 5 4 3 2 1

∞ This book is printed on acid-free paper.

Library of Congress Cataloging-in-Publication Data
Murray, G. E., 1945–
Arts of a cold sun : poems / by G. E. Murray.
p.   cm.
ISBN 0-252-02833-3 (cloth : alk. paper)
ISBN 0-252-07119-0 (pbk. : alk. paper)
I. Title.
PS3563.U768A88   2003
811'.54—dc21   2002010965

Acknowledgments

Grateful acknowledgment is made to the editors of the following publications where earlier versions of these poems first appeared:

Ascent: "Hide and Seek"
Boston Literary Review: "Speculation in Dark Air Smoking"
Chariton Review: "Apparitions, Approximations, Appearances," "Clearances," "Elizabeth Goose in Autumn," "North Beach Sweet," "Skibbereen Deeds," "Tales of the Weather"
Illinois Review: "At Les Deux Magots Restaurant"
The Madison Review: "Unclaimed Freight"
New American Writing: "At the Lifeboat Races," "Marginal Extravaganzas," "Opus Focus"
Notre Dame Review: "Anointing the Unprepared," "Chronicle of Choices"
Oxford Review: "Notes for the Interior Escape," "The Rainy Season Arrives in Southern Kyushu"
Poetry Now: "At the Club Hula," "Dispensations for an Afternoon Rain"
Rhino: "To the Dogs"
Rust Belt Review: "An Oral History of the East Side," "City without Archipelago," "Fanfare for a Cocktail," "High on the Flats," "Love in the Solarium," "Manholes," "Midnight Symphonies," "River through the City," "Trespasses"
The Sewanee Review: "Art of a Cold Sun," "Bugatti's Zoo," "True Stories about Color"
Slant: A Journal of Poetry: "The Unsung Song of Harry Duffy"
Story Quarterly: "At the Corner Bar at the End of Idle Street"

Sulphur River Literary Review: "In Praise of Invisibility," "Moon Snow,"
  "Facts about Unlucky Times"
Tamaqua: "The Seconds" (all 13 parts)
TriQuarterly: "Crawfordsville Confidential"
Willow Review: "Long Story Short"

To Mary Heffron Murray—
Mother, Model (role and fashion),
Reader and Teacher of the Love of the Word

Contents

The Seconds

Codes toward an Incidental City

One: Cold Sun

True Stories about Color

I leave you with these true stories about color
and its darkest adaptations:
how the eye gains by reduced illumination,
how maximum luminosity shifts
toward the blues of blood heat,
while yellow induces fever,
and purple flames deep like a beet. Or taxi black.
Or rain gray. Or greenheart hardwood.
It's never quite right or the same.

But more: that chilling look in the eyes
of infants or hurricanes: fate's vermilion,
burnt umbers of chance . . . dancing indigo . . . hazel ways.

The point in all this: the need to believe
in possessions becoming acceptable. Desires
coveting registration, numbered carefully
like colors, become only half the story
through all this, this intersection of three memories:

the pure-white courage of the duelist's front foot;
perpetual black in a patched eye;
sensational blues true to scars and veins laid open.

Van Gogh thought the *laws* of colors
unutterably beautiful
just because they are not *accidental*.
I would say *innocence*
in most colors is predictable as sex . . .
and the religion of art as trustworthy
as a sleepwalking gambler afraid of his own darks.

At the Lifeboat Races

Jersey, Channel Islands

Seeking the alibi of one vast unmixable shade of blue,
something between Jaguar-
approved metallic and that very dark,
almost black, bottomless color
the British Navy calls "Blue 3346."

An optical cliché
or storm-borne sky,
blue-gray as integrity.

At the annual lifeboat races,
and its concert by the sea,
a thing of shining and floating resolve
deep tunnels toward Poonah Lane,
conducting the night filling to melodies
with a toss of a 50 p. cigar.

Lightweight changes and charges,
reputations at stake—
involuntary guesses and refusals:

circling as one, as an idea blueing,
mirror-frozen,
like staring into the eye of a chicken.

Speculation in Dark Air Smoking

In Lugano, among lost paintings

You've come now, haven't you, playing on a bad knee,
unable to shake the feeling of an aphrodisiac for breakfast.
Thus dream with your eyes stuck open,
hot for conclave and analogue, the exquisite deal.

On an empty morning like this,
know about something
that will melt you beyond restitution
or the recourse of a middlebrow portfolio.
Know old works serve best
when they haven't been cleaned.
Know well those absurd meanings
of harsh words tossed about Thyssen Mansion,
where in room after room so many saintly paintings
take possession of you and the thief
curled in your heart as a worm,
conforms to your own irregularities.
Know that, and something less.

Now we move just one moment shy
of whatever happens from our time here together,
from proper imaginings that truly live on
in strokes of such unsuspecting reality.

Discovering landscapes by the spadeful
in long rooms over water, you in shades and leather,
primed for views of curiosity and extended
lending. I was about to leave on vacation
from light incarnate and the aroma of inevitability
when you called.

Art of a Cold Sun

I realize the horse seen from an airplane looks like a violin,
though it is more and otherwise . . . seizing
gives a shape to jealousy,
to make-believe sins of off-key laughter,
as if hiding a mouse
in my vest pocket . . . all of a piece
from the sun's rude nightly defection.

One must judge much junk before it becomes someone's art.
Ever consider the heretical impulse
as prologue to new orthodoxy,
complicated as a hair.

How plausible an eye that could herd scorpions.
In feral ways, marble-mouthed,
you come to think of it,
art's enlightenments
and the sting of its tail.

Apologies and claims made.
Warnings and promises issued.

Time won't lie, but it'll wink.

Anointing the Unprepared

In one disconsolate town, among many rhythms
now shutting down for second thoughts, you believe
in both the theory and the plumbing,
as well as any truths behind winning numbers.

At times, you become the period to the last paragraph.

Wistfully provincial, and ready to calculate
the effects of popular statistics, you wish
you could, like a French priest, smoke in church—

this in praise of abstracted spirits
on a cold spring day in Strasbourg. No question
about it, no worthy way to proceed
as if only a few lonely notes struck on a piano,
jinxed by darkling, instructive times.

Come the winter season and its need for deep
listening, you leave directions
on how to explain the dissolution
of boundaries among us. There are conditions
galore for our rattlings and tremors,

for the suspense of debris in the mirror.
Schisms necessarily implicate.
Dogmas resound. Always protocols elsewhere.

Who loses what when we have more teeth than we need?

Le Corps Bleu

Busy and bored as an angel, back to the cypress-lined coast,
returning as facsimile of the original.

Face down in serious pleasure,
a troubled sky's yellow domination laid out—

too rich to be unkind. I don't lead with the stray stuff
of memory's hard-ons. Rather,

I paint water into a ball and clever clouds
as water, favoring the painter's license

to practice fate: splicing familiars
to a new concentration of what's sacred about love

and its demarcations. With a morning moon
now slipping toward the cold storage of mid-harbor,

as both signature and hex. I hijack myself from my strokes,
piecemeal, scheming out of context. I'd even play

left-handed if only to gain speed
between the hand's eye and one eye's uncounseled argument.

You can snap all that in the back of your hat.

At Les Deux Magots Restaurant

At *Les Deux Magots* Restaurant,
conversation slips toward the void,
like a lizard wedged
into a crack in the wall.

It's the level of access achieved over time
that counts.
It's looking at love without ending
in stiches.

I think you've lost it
although I get the picture.

When we departed, a stain
delineating where we'd been,
hushed and etiolated—
went someplace, but will return.

Hide and Seek

Peeling away skins of the promise
as if Euro notes,
making the unknown seen
maunder in multiple ways. It's rumored Cézanne
had insomnia the night he died,
talking to Rembrandt's ghost, as if nothingness
contained a special *métier.* Funny how
what's left of the wicked and sweet
heart and tongue of madness comes
with a guarantee of art that looks
like art, not merely another incredible
bug in the eye.

How much could happiness cost anyway,
as it escapes into you, escapes me, pooh-poohed
as if love on a glass slide.

Elizabeth Goose in Autumn

For Megabeth

This far too soon into that late afternoon graying.
Thus, the ghostly season assembles once more.

How terribly sweet of you to be here now:

ancient as smoke, disguised as a sigh,
my Halloween schemer beaming
anticipation and aftermath: *Duck, Duck, Goose:*

your namesake game played out slippery among leaves,

while the half-orange night rises spellbound
to shade and echoes hauntingly
cold enough for these fatherly shivers.

How suddenly the soon-hereafter mystifies sincerely

in the wake of windows soaped, pumpkins smashed,
until your fine wordfoolery: *Zip, zap, zolla*—
incantation for a gathering of secret smiles.
Bewitched, as if one hour soaked in color,
we surrender to shadows divinely wicked,

ever sure. Dare-stare or pout, let's deny
each other early frost, leaving wet street
to other treats and tricks. So you conjure
new realm, and then disappearance: *Kaboosh!*

So again within our weathers, nothing else
tonight but news of the dark's dispensations . . .
Time now to venture out from under these great eaves

during autumns lost forever to hard rain from Paradise.

South of Spain

I was climbing this lemon tree looking for breakfast

there in the crux of suspect times.
My concessions minor and assumptions near gone,
troubling only over the sureness of ledges.

Pretend I'm not here suffering fate's scrapes,
hanging on as I am, believing already
in enough delusions of adequacy and wit—
that's too much the interior grope.

Notice now the trials of a man chasing up a tree,
a man in the isolation business,
who doesn't know the rules, much less any facts.

I trust that
circumstances of the phenomenal
bring on a higher limb of mind.
Under cold sun, amid side winds, reaching out
after what's low-hung and chosen,
falling—ah, but one bite short
of the eternal.

Long Story Short

One marriage, three children, the usual hero-to-hump tale
of jobs in alternating altitudes, stories of unrequited joy.
Fresh identities, dramas unseen. Too much of dawn
going dark, making for a rich meal of dread, when contemplating
love above the brim.

You also should talk about dealings with heavy weather
and one-night agonies, as if descending permanently
into a single distinction. It boils to skin
and plain whim, or any fabrication sufficient
to implicate the act.

Just then, something glimpsed from a taxi careening
through Paris, afterimages of a lost father's face
becomes a tree in the park, tall, rustling with allusions,
or was it simply cool air stealing across your face—
that isolation again?

To the Dogs

After Buster

Times when the starting gate closes
too fast and hard on my tale
only prove me slow to the bone

in trophy worlds of fetch and sic.

I'd wager the trifecta,
bet the unmuzzled bloodline, being
a wheel-chaser at heart, cold bark at dawn,

afraid at last to outrun the faux rabbit.

I'll see you backstretch. I'll bite
a bit. I'll circle and circle until
I feel it's time to put down instinctively—

late last days now counted in dog-years.

Notes for the Interior Escape

The receding eyehole,
a hairy loss.

These failed coordinates
leave you lost
at the sight of another exit gate.

To go unnoticed:
always keep a shadow
your very size beside you.
Glide smart and dark
down unmarked rivers,
cool and anonymous.

Never lean all one way
when flirting
with genuine silence or light,
monumental stones,
even blizzards. Turn meek,

quiet enough to blossom alone
or participate fully
as a replacement part
for good luck or taste.

The real trick turned:
enter a seascape canvas
as one tiny self-portrait
you would be rid of:
shy as a lapping wave,
soft as church music,
inconceivable as oceans.
Then paint over often.

The Rainy Season Arrives
in Southern Kyushu

This afternoon the color of twine
blown free as hair.

Otherwise ever fading in an afterward,
behind waterfall
and among occupations of a long pause
slipped tight between kisses.
Love's major accessories work hardest
off-axis, too dear in miniature.

Then the rubbing of edges.
Then such utterance.

All hairs wet down
while dreaming beautiful excesses
of light burning
immaculate on the Yellow Sea.

Rain's first puzzlements:
unpredictability and inconsistency:
modern mist hung amid drowning stones.

Clearances

On the Shores of Lake Erie

Years back there were stories of the lake burning late
and dead-wrong rumors of wolves
beating slack-jawed through cattail cover
over by Sunset Beach. And overnight, always,
time enough to get the tellings right. It was all constant
surprise to those who saw nothing and understood
less. Oh, a small fire perhaps, flashings
spilled from a cracked freighter. But absolutely
no trace of wolf, unless you count
those inexplicable accidents of garbage randomly
strewn down Dunkirk Road like pelts. Still,
each year, fewer and fewer of the regular beach people
remember when and why to return . . .

. . . Instinctively, far out in the Western Reserve,
other alarms and stirrings, if only pre-dawn calls
for cold cereal or lovemaking. Morning haze
floods an expansive back lawn croquet field,
lifting gradually from abandoned mallets and hoops,
rock-hard balls lost among hyacinths.
Another day slim as a chance, raw as nerves.
In early April, solitary weeks linked
by problems with the pump-house and that radio static
crackling off the lake, asking for points
of clearance: Silver Creek, Port Credit, Sandusky
and farther west, following carp
and the implausible surge and tug of the steel routes.

Never mind the folklore of loss you collect
around town like groceries and parking tickets—
hearsay of dogs lost to undertow, unconfirmed reports

of midnight collisions on back roads surely
untraveled. But it's only natural, the usual
defense against one lake's pitch and draw,
against seiche. Stars continue brilliant everywhere
until late August. Advising how little we guess
about hidden curves, curses, some breeze-cooled idea
looming inches ahead of headlights swerving home.
Not that it matters much to anyone not lost out here,
out past breakwater, this swallowing of all that mist touches,
those dark poplars hissing back at the piecemeal night.

All this survives without warning. Regular enigmas
of summer's morning shore without redemption—a toddler
amused by nothing so irrational as its own shadow at noon.
Maybe there's hell in the bones
of those bathing here. Blood fired by such sun—
dumb and anonymous. Anything could erupt
beyond bearing, if only for impatience. Cherish,
then, the scene of horn-honking tourist boats
steaming out through the channel water's dazzling,
grasp of safe harbor or another ketchup-smeared face,
blue wash unfurling toward far sunset.
Each scattered in the names
of radiance and disappointment.

You still don't know if peace of mind was ever part
of the agreement you made with clouds—rippled
and dappled. You and a child must explain to each other
the dead smelts, each having lived, each part
of shore and home. Eye of the fish stares
clear, fixed among sand castles,
steady as last night's roadhouse promise.
The beach becomes indifference and confirms
answers of belief: that's all that's known
about the fail-safe life in summer's grotto.
No wonder hundreds today outwit the sun's gaze,
set fast in plots, affairs and driftings
against reef, backwash, incomplete distances.

Sunset. Then the cool black liquid air advances
as either perfume or hazard. Or artistry
too strong to realize its own twists. A breeze swells up,
turning south, missing you this tin can–colored night.
Neon crackles over by Sunset Beach. High winds
press against the aging Ferris wheel. Poof-poof—
fake rounds from the shooting gallery, its Kewpie dolls
propped up, a cheap and cheerful version of heaven. Beer voices
hover bonfires on the beach, dune whispers,
strings plucked, and lake freighters passing through a wrong century.
Cheers, then applause. Someone chooses a mallet
to begin the play of midnight's croquet. Smack!
Do you hear a howling inland?
Do you really need to see the lake catch fire to believe it?

Skibbereen Deeds

On our way to one Mrs. Minihane's occasional pub in Skibbereen
—the Lotto capital of Ireland—
we go chasing the Minihane (or Minnehan) DNA that is us,
roaming this strip of West Cork turf—
forever wild and unkempt as a cowlick.

Our grandmother's place of birth and departure.
How in God's hell does a young girl
circa 1890 get from here to Cobh Harbor,
much less New York City and beyond? Mrs. Minihane guesses,
Like most of them. By mule and foot and by luck.

With luck, we too will travel again before twilight.
But only after a prowl of this mystic coast,
solemnly seeking connection, with Mike and Tim
climbing fence and thicket, staggering through graveyards,
as we paused many times on lost roads driving down from Bantry.

Mrs. Minihane admits she's only lived in Skibbereen
for sixty years or so. So she wouldn't have known our Catherine,
or, here, was it young Kate? But looking at Tim,
she volunteers, *You look just like Rory Minihane,*
who runs the woolen mill outside of town.

Would we plod down to the mill and make fools
of ourselves? No. Would we speculate and wonder
what tales of exit and return were set free to wander? Yes.
And construe dislocation and passage elsewhere?
And then, otherwise, the need to travel for survival? Surely.

Ah, elaborate routes to roots. How American of us,
to hope capturing our temporary shadows.
Instead, there is a fine, grinding emptiness to all this—
out looming out after histories so minor
only a handful of lovers will find them compelling or useful.

The dream of reading a truth or two into transformations
from the vacancy of this ground
propels us toward self-pronouncement, pint by pint.
The unresolved still accumulates.
The blank looks, the tight mews walks, still beg answers.

Yet a sharp, cooling wind makes everything possible
when perfectly at home, we say. The exhaustion
from such restless excavations abides.
What more remains than to find the ancient church
where she said her first prayers.

And we did, at last, by nothing more than tough
luck's edge. Maybe touching such nerves, luck means
this lifetime appointment of ambiguities,
this wind-shifting irrelevance,
this late acknowledgment of consequence.

Again, rummaging among so many personal bone-fields
and digging out curious nineteenth-century tales
before turning our own tails eastward,
we dance among the traditional Irish dangers
of birth cries and lively wakes.

Mrs. Minihane draws more Guinness and allows how,
*It's a lucky town now, but hasn't always been
that way.* In the far, homing country stimulating
backbone and foothold, this story turns
mythic itself—both dear and damning, so

we can now touch those demons in our own saints, and in us.

North Beach Sweet

For the one son, Michael

> But you, from this side of your time,
> How do you live, poet.
> How much fuel do you have left for the trip
> You wanted replete with seagulls?
> —Julio Cortazar

1.

You sometimes get upside-down here faster than a seagull
dive-bombing the unassuming and often betrayed,
observing the loosey-goosey and heroin chic
dialectic, as we jostle to joke
about hanging tough and far long while adrift,
out making rounds of the lost bars
as if praying the Stations of the Cross.

"That's the spot where Kerouac yaked, Jack,"
goes the tourist buzz at Vesuvio Lounge. Now is good.
Now is painless as researching the right tattoo parlor
or the very nature of techtonic shifts.

Hard to guess what's quotidian these days,
but we do know Columbus Avenue opens wide at both ends

to mysterious histories of mad dogs in the fog.

2.

The brothers DiMaggio played great stickball here—
Dom, Joe, Vince, and us too,
each elegant on the dead run.
Blast a ball hard as you possibly can
blue sky–high to see whatever
the gods of bay breezes will do with it—

as if only blowing jazz, hey what, say
Turk Murphy, Jeru Mulligan, the Teagardens also
blew straight-set sessions in this place,
like sweet evening rain
that also wouldn't quit. Truth is,
truth was or will be. But we invent more
left-coast sideshows, listening
to rags unsuitable for any but the finest ears
primed late night at the Washington Square Bar and Grille.

Outside, seagulls still cry lullabies.
That much is real.

3.

This shining day, precursor to a fine aria
filled with roulades and trills,
as if film noir music, exaggerating distance
between notes, melody sailing higher
than counter-intuitive accompaniment,
in this city of sopranos.

No buy-in on gull-diving bluffs
or cloud-splitting ways of a flap-run,
it's our great 360° roll. In these times we trust
the upside-downness of such cutting-edge advice:
keep your best blades oiled and keep them
out of the weather.

4.

All by way of absolute originals
in this next hour together,
North Beach's newest innkeeper
Myles O'Reilly bids adieu
to father and son and that grand idea
of gliding out of one hole
into another. Winds stiffening
as a trumpeter's lip

slipping off a last high note.
So what's about jazz
and its negotiations,
colorations and journeys,
so what's this crazy about words
being seagulls
rising, and rising as if thrills
swooping to us so elegantly on the dead run.

Bugatti's Zoo

Not only did World War I force Rembrandt Bugatti to abandon his
work as an animal sculptor, but because of the war, all "his friends"
vanished. The animals of the Jardin Zoologique in Brussels were
slaughtered because they could no longer be fed. Shortly thereafter,
Rembrandt Bugatti, 31, poisoned himself with gas.
—Bugatti catalog, The Cleveland Museum of Art

(Entries from Bugatti's notebooks)

I live to release continuance and the velocity of cunning

in my sacred menagerie
in loving bronze
in Antwerp. Vultures and deer,

yak, tapir, ostrich, cassowary and baboon,
along with hippopotami, lions—
gudu and emus. Very pure, very fine,

happiness in Florentine details.
The secretary birds now seize my attention.
A wild rooster also beckons. Who could ever imagine,

more than I, the endless elegance of the dziggetais?

  ✳ ✳ ✳

If you drop focus only a touch, someone else takes advantage.
Behind the mask of the particulars
of omnipotence and ignorance,
there is nothing really irreverent,
nothing at all ever again
without consolation
and misunderstood translation,
shaped by well-earned darks of destiny.

What pleases, what devours,
easily comes undone as a peace treaty.

    *   *   *

I stand hidebound
by the world's sideshows.
Out of chances, bleak
as Belgium in March.
I count upon failures
to be special blessings.
Life happens when
you dream other things,
still guessing, guessing.
My testimony is about
tails and horns and hooves
and the beatitudes
of beasts, exact and warm
as the inward wind
I so miss in my veins.

    *   *   *

When winter never leaves (or lives),
one misting evening I went lost
between Groenplatts und Zickstraat—
insatiably unable to grow old,

when even my elephants forgot where to go
to die.

The Unsung Song of Harry Duffy

Pure veins of bogus blue-blood and such fancy hungers

~

In the end no surprise of reports of you dying younger than your gods

~

Kicked back in the classic toilet scene

~

With a spike in your arm and twelve large in pocket

~

Thanks to a lucky day scamming the dumb Social Services folks

~

It's a human thing, pants at your ankles, leaving unclean

~

Because life's road is only one night in a bad motel

~

Harry, you could play basketball in your bare feet, and win

~

You could name all the provinces of Canada

~

And simultaneously scour the Social Register

~

For the names of those sad and silly girls you wanted to get right

~

You relished autumn leaves and ignited inglorious schemes

~

Deconstructing the idea of prep-school Friday sunsets

~

In lavish October, stealing among faculty hors d'oeuvres and sherry

~

All the while creating your own hooligan oeuvre

~

With your others off to Yale, Colgate, Brown

~

Night after night, alone in L.A.

~

Seeking better quotas, vistas, cushion, heroin

~

And that last tricky exit to the Santa Monica Freeway

~

In one more borrowed car with one more borrowed fiction

~

Oh yes, you must have been laughing

~

And spitting back at the boldface of Pacific wind

~

Cruising the left coast on sheer gall

~

But mostly, at 3 A.M., in the local playground, Harry

~

You played solitary ball

~

And dreamed of final seconds in a distant game

~

You drove to the sacred bucket with a fury

~

Slick crossover dribble, and then burst to the pull-up jumper

~

No harm, no foul, nothing but net.

~

But all alone, in the heart of West Hollywood, Harry,

~

You jerk, you bricked the last shot.

Crawfordsville Confidential

1.

In the land of milk and cream delivered early
and daily, and always in glass bottles, we care
about good grooming and, of course, news
of slurs and curs . . . Can it really be that home

becomes a place to be stranded?
"I don't see a single storm cloud
anywhere in the sky, but I can sure smell rain,"
out on the edge of Crawfordsville, Indiana,
where the answers and questions become identical
as evil twins.

2.

Basketball ghosts bounce and sweat again
in that second-floor gym in the middle of July—
that never-to-be-forgotten home
of the first-ever Boys State Championship.
Rusty jump shots and long-ago corner hooks
rim out in a stream of dusted sunlight.
"Just to play the game, don't you know,
you know, no matter how much the sacrifice . . ."
How searing afternoon's vagueness now,
dreamed in a daylong haze of headache pills
downed at the General Lew Wallace Motor Lodge:
how the arc of the ball rises
to echoes of split-jump cheers
in lubricated air, when phantom bodies
strive and leap and go prostrate

to that squeak of rubber on polished wood—
in a game of shirts and skins.

3.

You can only wonder how Ezra Pound dissected his time here,
among tractors and proctors and temples of antebellum style,
as he cooed sweet Greek in the ear
of his secular Madonna . . . Just now, two pigeons
greet first daylight on the Green of Wabash College.

Something to be said for being scandalized silly,
and in more than one language
when life becomes holier than the Crusades.
And what's more—didactic passions
eventually drive you insane, thinks young EP, so what?
Sew buttons, ha!

And make it new always . . . and always
leave the door cracked open, a light on,
and one foot on the floor.

4.

"The meatloaf here's not very good,"
warns waitress Lucy, a pretty girl
with a tooth missing. Indifferently,
day proceeds utterly.
Off Country Road X-10, out by Carcus Creek,
driving past Minnie Betts's florist shop
and what's left of the old city jail,
you figure each small detail adds
glory to any story.
                "Relax," says Elton Bidwell,
the county's dead-buzzard collector,
"I'll take care of us all
when we com' on home."

5.

The town goes dark in a killer storm.
Collective forgetting and forgiving
occurs. But safety comes in many forms.
In this vast black you get to thinking
about giddy joys and little sorrows,
the curse of full employment at minimum wage,
and those conspicuous professors—
their bowties and braces speaking to the ages
and marking moments of learned unworthiness.
Maybe, it's vacuum-packed fear
in a stage-managed town. Time to guess
what's behind each tiny crime and local leer,
at once rancorous and baffling. Strangers
need not apply. A few lights click on
at the Shortstop Grille. These cruel weathers
turn asphalt slick. The old intramurals begin again.

6.

Early Sunday morning and a drunken Elton Bidwell
is strung like a scarecrow on his front porch swing,
deposited by Grand Wizards from the Odd Fellows Lodge bar
late last night—reminder to those devoted folks
heading up Church Street with songbooks in hand,
that home sure proves just another place to be stranded.

The Seconds

A Note on "The Seconds": Contemplating Atmospheres

The premise of "The Seconds" is to seize a moment's temperament, elusiveness, and temperature on a certain day—the second—of each month for a full year. Thus, "The Seconds" is a sequential poem given to the *moment's* value and the *instant's* veracity.

Call these poems *hatchings:* ways to delve into circumstance and emotion with immediacy. The thirteen sections of "The Seconds" are variously influenced by *atmospheres,* which by broad definition engage climate and mood as well as disturbances in reception. Also in force here are those insistent edges that become tastes, desires, faith, touches. And weights and waits.

The Seconds

December Second

Early, cold
   light of tin
angels. Us hauling a year's weight
   now dusted
and nearly deceased. So pray
   for release
from the glee quota that doesn't
   hold. Christmas
approaching. Coming in horizon-low,
   those forces
under seasonal wind or radar screen.
   Time to signal
general quarters.

January Second

Ice forming from my sleep. ZZZZ.
   Winter surfacing
      as a book of snow.
ZZZ. Under gun,
      hotel-bound,
      feelings unfinished,
all communications sealed. ZZ.
   January darks
      notching down
to empty depths. Now wisely go on
   hibernating. Z.

February Second

In the lee of an empty room,
a wink eventually becomes a twitch.

    Contents under pressure:
    delusions of safety,
    whispers and defections
    gone secret. Snow suddenly
    whips Michigan Avenue white.

I think of the hardening causes
of muscle, Central Time, scientific praises.

    With my skin humming,
    this instant blanks
    to the bleak sincerely,
    the heart oversized, leaking
    at last, uncommonly.

Then in the song of the empty room,
accidents unloved, perfected later perhaps.

March Second

Struck dumb by an obscurity,
bamboozled by the lure
of body English. Going once, twice.
Overheard, an unknown tongue,
less sure of hocus-pocus
than usual, than a gray-morning ache
for some bottomless number.
This very day turns cruel as a nursery rhyme.

April Second

A wetness sprung from stone under high-roller clouds.
I come to love this trail through the actual.

Temperatures still raw. Sounds still proud.
There's a pleasure to be gained in authenticity,

in the first jazz-notes of spring, quick and truant
as habits. Take shelter from a proper angle

on who's in the offing or over the top.
In a pre-dawn speech you claim the trill

of Miles Davis remains ever pressed,
thin and suspect as the hide of a hummingbird.

May Second

This sureness of edge,
the jackknifed life.
Running under a caution flag
flying lakeside
as holy remembrance,
so a true north bearing
can serve as our extra brain.

Fast track, hiking out
on boat rails, slick water
reaching toward insouciance.
So the act becomes
young and customary
as accomplices and urges.

This lathering, that cut.
Such a French gesture.

June Second

Incurable necessities
against memory
stand down now
among fastballs

that get lost in the high weeds,
ever on a string.
Give chase to greater games,

to souvenirs and swaggers,
to bad news from the outfield,

knowing it always gets dark here too late.

July Second

That circling proceeds with assurances,
and this instant of connection
on death day. My late father twists

in a wind-blown curtain,
as a clarinet hails cliché truth,
as if the precise mistake you ordered.

Lucky for us the sun
also sets; us still steam-bent.
Champions know best how ice works in heat.

August Second

Huffed and straddled
among travelers
in Alphabet City,
feeling delinquent
to hot-brained hurries,
and passwords and blue moons,
each ridiculously beautiful;
and me, thinking beach,
thinking distance and desire,
just getting the hang of it all
that's delicious, private and rising

on less than an average planet.

September Second

      Make way
or weigh in. Last chance for linen
   suits and sheer pluck
harborside. This day pours like music
      among undecided realities.
      Anchor the eye
to lush loneliness, sailboats gliding
   northerly, spinnakers rising
      full-hearted, drunken
      balloons. Even
in ruins, love that ripens all around
   you, leaves much unsaid
in the vacant present . . . Soon,
      lesser times.

October Second

Oarlocks cranking alive before
dawn takes the Charles River
with deep, repeated phrases
for the unlistening ear . . .

Cruising the skin of the scene
this captured day,
I shoot a look into the shadows
on shore, air bristling
over there, in the bushes

and beyond. Something's busted
free in the dark—love's knot
unraveling, sacred mist lifting
from that dream discontinued again.

November Second

       Bitter autumn
evening, near the end of a story
    you finished long ago but anonymously.
       In the company
of fog, night turns colder, the cold
    darker and, more seriously,
       dislocated. Oh,
comic memories of blood and stitches,
    that wounded-stag look now
       appearing heroically
stupid in old football leather,
    not yet stunned enough,
    not yet the unstoppable self.

December Second Again

Dear holiday receptions and sweet anticipations
beg seasonal inculcation against proposition
and a holy consignment of weather. Give me mine.

Chunks of me agree with early sunset and suitable
retreat to vestibules and anterooms

of old stone places. Chilly syllables hardly left
to chance. I love first snow and those fists of snow
only now decreed absolute and sacrosanct

as that odd flutter of some bluebird escaping
from the woodwork, out of season and control.

No need yet to put a hard name on incarnation
in times of parting and silence. Hail Mother,
I'm full of ghosts and sweats and casualties,

wondering whether to make much of little
or little of much that goes unredeemed.

Codes toward
an Incidental City

I will feel lost,
unhappy and at home.
—Seamus Heaney

You always know where you
come from, don't you?
—Robert Frost

Up the index of night, granite and steel
—Hart Crane

The way I enter a city barefoot and end
up in a luxurious flat . . .
—James Joyce

So the inner city emptied of everything but people.
—Kai Erikson

A Note on "Codes toward an Incidental City"

In its shards and dispatches, this city assembles itself as no particular place to go and no one place you have ever been. It's the city prescribed as elixir drawn from what's equally familiar and fabulous. It is again the city as entanglements of circumstance and mishap.

The city as silence, at 4 A.M., a few raindrops still adding to a puddle in the parking lot of a just-closed nightclub or industrial site now coming to life across town. The intersection of the night watchman and the baker rising predictably before dawn. Then the many incomprehensible dances in that actual world that deliver answers without questions. Whether contemplating the planning of a near-perfect heist. Or confounded by the suddenness of a broken pipe. Or what's defined simply by reports of traffic and weather, and all that surfaces near the high end of what's decreed as average. Or perhaps old blood mingling toward a new alias. Or, best of all, the expandable night eventually saved by the wisdom of an unturned doorknob.

1. In Praise of Invisibility

Of waitresses and messengers and window-washers
thirty stories up
night's index of steel and glass,
who's most expert in the pretense of absence?

Never forget, obligations of champagne
are deeply felt, luxuriously sincere

as someone from a penthouse perch
insists on a dab of brie.

Distinctions without differences.

In aftermath, know only this:
unobserved,
the finest servants
fear no one.

2. Chronicle of Choices

Times coming now to resuscitate genius
or go sure and improvise
among souvenirs of dislocation,
or what's left of buzzard's luck,
or failing that,
wet any finger that beckons wind
to articulate direction. Ah,

that stillness of waiting, not yet of death—
as only unlikely turns make perfect sense.

You—amused by the randomness
of weather—will cling to home brews,
while a luminous snow cover
serves as rationale for the resistance

in this City of No Illusions,
carefully situated
ever next to nowhere,
where being proud
doesn't matter
anymore.

3. City without Archipelago

Let's pretend to tell you
how ordinary this topology appears,
how nondescript the avenues
how profane in their swiftness,
how natively sublime,
how scarce in our durations,
how perfectly essential
each inconsequential dawn
when this place falls silent as a god.

4. Tales of the Weather

Storm front forming late into a bruise—
like Monet's *Waterlilies*—
awash in purple and green.

This weather turns sudden and truly dark ·
as a maiden's autumn statement.

Be grateful that more isn't asked of you.

5. Used News

In future reference to those remains
exquisitely caught within the switches:
first get those cold facts fixed

because everything must be recorded:
a reverence for what's remembered;
our splendid embarrassments,

assumptions gone mystical;
even time spent as love
at the Empty Arms Motel.

Or simply the praise of rain—
straight and hard as the elms
that grow old on gossip alone.

6. Dispensations for an Afternoon Rain

Sometimes all that remains proves the doorknob.

Or, up for anything—
two distant figures preparing
to dissolve into steam-bath mist.
Or the deviations of Lady Chardonnay
ensconced in a dark mahogany corner
at Chez Steak, awaiting
the next echelon. Divine distractions

prevail as you peek out
between curtains, study the skyline,
with little appetite for what's shade-grown.
How to make up for being
late and given to interpretation?
The TV mutters continually.
The mail is overdue again.

7. Darkening Probabilities

Beautiful losers stalk holy grounds.

Indifference becomes the only relief
when strolling boulevards
lost to warning and instruction,

yet surely policed by a wide smile

as innocence perpetuates itself
within high-ceilinged rooms. Elsewhere,
crutch-thieves and ankle-biters

assemble in search of a stubborn otherness.

Living on the cheap, among
famous parks and better schoolyards,
why more focus on more?

Being in too far already to get out, you guess.

8. Moon Snow

That yellow-gray dusk of winter takes a stab
at blank astonishment and gets it right.

Under an ailing moon,
it's time for crewel work
that has new meaning.

Ancient hatreds lay low tonight.
No sanctions, only cease-fires,
and little enough to boast about

with snow becoming most influential again.

9. The Story of Minus

For Richard Martins

City kids skilled in killing do much of the dying,
often cursed with half a smile.

The answer now is *What?*

Put a decent face on our diminishings
and muckheaps, our meanings abysmal,

incomprehensible to even ourselves

as we lie awake staring in the air-conditioned dark,
counting our subtractions.

Nihil subteranae est.

10. Marginal Extravaganzas

I took on the incognito job
to search a science for the Whammy.
I began haunting the wig and nail and resale shops,
seeking the right selection of nostrums.

I looked to a book of quaint philosophies
to appreciate ways of morphing from enticements
to scar tissue, from gains recalibrated
to irretrievable fates.

Entre nous, these days it's all either
downloaded or deferred,
eccentric skies or rueful days,
feeling at home being lost.

11. Homing

Right you are, left it is—
    these pigeons going off again apropos
        of city souls adrift,
on hard wing, choir-like, high of mind and lift—

racing northeasterly with rooftop secrets
    as songlines and extremities,
        half-captive, half-fugitive,
gliding against a smoke-stacked skyline.

Are solemn gray days part of the calculation,
    this periscope scan,
        as adventures diminish
to hoping at least one bird opts for a wrong turn

and sprints free?

12. Facts about Unlucky Times

The performing sciences
offer proof conclusive:

pain becomes art,
art begets investment

and a city dying
looks deep into its archives

for wrongdoing
and fractured syntax.

Here, tomorrow's
often Monday

and too many hearts continue
to seek residuals.

You don't have much of an edge
unless someone falls off.

Tragic riddle or distraction?
In solemn miscommunication with a future,

please understand: occasionally you find
nail polish inside a fist.

13. Opus Focus

As misty expectations clear out bell-like, there comes
an assemblage of disorderly ideas
about what defies treatment
of the city's phonic and acoustic
instincts, susceptible to demonstration
of incontestable crap and subject
to views that vary from street to haggard street.

Double-up on obstinate inertia,
ordinary damages,
accumulated dangers.

What gets absorbed while the remarkable occurs
in the mind of someone not wholly there?

14. Occupant

Noticeably nameless
and happily lost in a shell game,
notoriously absent—

able to avoid indictment,
explanation or induction, mastering
the blind exit,

embraced only by factlessness,
safe as if all of a vanishing kind
of that lucky clan known as the unknowns.

Secreted away like an Easter egg,
nothing personal,
of course, unregistered, delisted,

misplaced as a childhood
played out in whiteface.
Technically, you are not truly a lie

or yet compromised enough to ever be seen.

15. Unclaimed Freight

This way to the unwanted.
As if your mind was topped by loops of razor-wire
guarding tonight that slender haul
of doggerel and excuses,

abandoned like tools in a primitive hut.

Down there on Iron Street, rough nights
and loot in that loft where

you made love incessantly
looking out over the industrial park
with its artifacts and illuminations
stashed among other municipal mementoes.

Confusing, eh?
Endlessly maze-like, as if playing a cameo
in *The Maltese Falcon*.

Who's got the dingus? Who even remembers
what it looks like?

16. River through the City

The itch to wave wildly
while boats and ducks
proceed as insinuations

will pass, eventually.
Benefits and burdens
become sweethearts,

casually observing
a flow of reinvention.
This quick, you go

bleak and gritty,
enough to become lyrical
and abandoned to jazz.

River of impartiality,
blissed out,
as it makes vital

intercessory prayer.

17. At the Club Hula

At the beginning of an unrefined afternoon
at Club Hula's weekly lipstick show,
a zero-sum game ensues
among these many moving parts
of those known as reliable witnesses
to the stark geometry of desire.
Hey drummer, a rim shot, pah-leeze,
for all that strips and wilts away
for the sake of naked complicity
for whomever shivers on the job
in light of delights,
in this succession of take-aways
around lunchtime. Snappy patter,
fallen wonders, city scratchings
hard-pressed and almost secret
as an exchange of looks
you seem too embarrassed to acknowledge.

18. Midnight Symphonies

One puddle mourning
midnight's symphony
in an empty parking lot
behind the long-haul terminal,
amid insurance

against heedless dreams—
when even shadows
go liquid and reflective,
and celebrate the day's first
splash!

19. High on the Flats

Dark murmur, then hurrah!
A new philosophy of giving at the office
down at the Mistake Exchange

promotes silly resentment
among the window-lickers
among us, left bad-mouthing

our influential skyline
from afar. Oh sweet ruins,
here below Tap City,

abandoned once more to poor form—
blue as pain—
but all for the good cause, or craze.

If all this seems untidy
as a pack of rampaging dogs,
then it's time for the natives to bite back.

20. Holed Up in the Old Hotel

Voices clanging through and out radiator pipes: best way to reach
you—you, clever as a fish in a bowl leaking water. Vague offers and
threats repeated often enough to consider the urge to descend into
disguise. Segue to the pseudo, and ever more tales of temptation and
trendy indecision. Outside, sounds of working people picking their
way through the previous night's detritus, the sibilant noise of
brooms on cement, the crash of glass flung in the gutter, that
whoosh of water sweeping away vomit and cigarette butts and pork-
rind bags—morning after morning.

By Friday, redundancy plagues even the desk clerk's squint. You too
find the dark ambience of the lobby sad. In near privacy, emotions
go numb and unedited. Except for the woman down the hallway re-
selling her Prozac. You trouble to rearrange furniture, but better yet
to have an exit strategy in mind. Yes, this is a good way to be hard-
wired to cool anonymity—yet so often you just run into juice-heads
and jamokes, fading in and out of the lobby, looking for cheap
conclusions. Sleep half the day, percolate all night. From experience,
you never keep real names or numbers on paper. Better to talk to
faces, while making the necessary arrangements as you stare down
from your window for hours on a summer night city, hot and
redolent. Otherwise, enough.

21. Apparitions, Approximations, Appearances

When and where even graffiti
has an agent, hobos don't beg—

they inquire. Millennium therapy

may be the first and only answer
to those blurring scars of logo removal.

There goes the neighborhood
again, as local history fast-forwards

to a quadrennial vision
of unsponsored humor and its vigorish.

You maintain the right to tell lies in all necessary languages.

22. At the Corner Bar at the End of Idle Street

There's been an overcoat left on a hook
in the back of the bar all summer long,
playing witness to the parade

of bald men on missions, one-off dreamers, noble nuns panhandling,
softball players and sponsors, and quitters and inquisitors, pig-nosed
mothers, crying slobs and mobbed-up guys, always a fine sampling
of the underaged. Pests and agents, exclusive users of the men's
room, worthy beauticians and their lovers. Grown men crying, new
blood and those unavailable for even the slightest conversation,
starring hard and straight into the mirror. Someone with a tinfoil
hat. Flops and average cops. Dog walkers, union-jacketed workers,
intense stalkers, intermediaries. A rabbi asking directions, a drop-out
giving directions. One professor. Two advertising executives. Three
friends. Whatever happened to the stiff who owned the new Jaguar
car? A full complement of bartenders, thank God. Even the
proprietor and his lovely niece show up occasionally.

Hey, who took the coat?

23. A Guide to Brief Encounters

By the week or pound
fictions whisper everywhere:
deceptions and interventions;
sweeps and searches,
the revenge of charity
turning another vintage.
What becomes ruckus?
That mistaken anticipation
at the Hotel Moonglow
was purely circumstantial.

New sobriquets and riffs
toward midnight. Later,
a wind that goes unpunished,
long-lost grunts of choice.
So shed another skin
instantly and watch out
for broken glass. Word
arrives by messenger
that love is feared dead
or at least quarantined.

24. Overnight

This evening's last cha-cha
at the Crystal Beach Pavilion ends, and so
begins the overnight shift
in other far dark corners, exactly

the opposite of your renowned fresh start.

While you think you think as you sleep,
what becomes bleak and unengaged
actually moves sideways, often aimlessly.

What is so destined
to go missing
should depart now—

as empty trains shuttle,
and neon boasts unnoticed,
and a steam valve hisses alone
and intemperately,

as you toss again, worrying again
about objects obtained, subjects voided,

during those fragile, nothing hours of night.

25. Metro Retro

Money is speech, or lack of it, as you grow increasingly
fond of the hum of an open phone line.

Another dawn becomes amendable.

Whether stranded in Boys Town,
Dark Town, Pill Hill, Dog Beach, et cetera

money is space and light and all that turns

rambunctious. You need to be filled
with something more than street smells

and an attitude, when money becomes speed

that can scan and sort us out
to astounding effect:

Ah, yes, a ringing silence in the city.

26. An Oral History of the East Side

With all the old stories disappearing
and the half-life on your anger starting to falter
in an instant everlasting,

you linger over a scene in which nothing is at stake,
except to perfect the ill-advised
and make yourself better known
to strangers unable to zigzag past your bench.

Beginning with accounts of that three-legged dog
saving the teacher's homework,
not to mention the longest fly ball ever hit
before or after The War on this or any continent,
or your take on bringing back
the quaint practices of sanctuary
and public execution.
Or why you tell anyone who'll listen,
"History's only as memorable
as a cramp . . ."

But always, always end up telling
why a lifetime here
makes incessant talking as necessary
as a fly swatter in summer.

27. The Arrangements

Statistical prophecies beget urban psalms.

On a dreadful and soggy Thursday morning
graveside, given to acquiescence
and simple subtraction, the pallbearers
pull on their gloves,

and move through the bereaved crowd
with business cards freshly inked.

28. Trespasses

"We have to win again soon
because it's been so long."

At six o'clock sharp the union lathes stop.
Frail engines urge on elsewhere.
The Children of Defeat
who forever toil upstairs
learn to appreciate
the continuing obbligato
of turbines and pumps,
rust and scars.

You know the warm breath of some liar on your neck.
You revel in the empowerment of emptiness.

29. Doubleheader: A Sonnet

Get wholesome and go immaculate.
The sacred musics of a new season,
the very next inning. Begin again daily surveillance
of green fields, curve balls, advertising
or ivy on those walls, soft winds off the lake.
Going blind to agate type every morning after.

Perfect. Keep it ready, edgy and regular.
Swap a few tales of age-old trivia—
the mythic numbers and names, say,
the last first baseman to ever kiss a catcher
or Babe Ruth's favorite bartender?
Love of the game: a straightjacket
for two. Or more. Or when.
But then, as always, superbly unfinished.

30. Jackhammer Blues

Deep skill of constant drilling
keeps it all unreal.

Every corner knows something different.

Deep skill of constant drilling
keeps it all unreal.

The demolition permit gets pulled again.

Deep skill of constant drilling
keeps it all unreal.

Maybe that's old sewer gas leaking?

Deep skill of constant drilling
keeps it all unreal.

Or just smells of coffee, concrete dust, and cigarettes.

Deep skill of constant drilling
keeps it all unreal.

In actual fact, the end of all this becomes the meantime.

31. Exhumations, Evictions, Evacuations

Late afternoon: the entr'acte between dusk and darkness
unveils the lackadaisical ways
sunset succumbs to charms at the Boulevard Mall.

Evening fills with conditional phrases
and unconscious borrowings
from the enormity of the ordinary,
as if stealing again from your mother's purse.

32. At the Bus Station

When my ship comes in, I'll probably be at the bus station.
—vaudeville humor

Fumes from distant buses rolling in with the dawn.

Plenty of dots coming and going and begging
not to be connected.

For all you know this corkscrewing
of faces becomes penetrating
and innocuous as radiation.
Wherever they go they scatter as evidence
of the actual and the inadmissible,

while the overnight temperature falls steadily.

33. Love in the Solarium

Soft, bulging curves with hard colors
indentured to the sky
and its make-over privileges.

That, and love already wind-dated,
given the widest possible latitude.

On the right track, looking
about a sadly odd place: testing
your own steam
in an exhibition space
of stone and glass and metal
catching the melting light
of a perpetually rainy city.

34. Civil Spaces

Drawn to Central Square this unintended night
when snow scrappers sweep the cobblestones
in a mechanized ballet. Everything you own is
captured by one black eye and a plastic bag.

You travel without visible means or a breakable habit

as the rabble size you up,
as the winds whipsaw only the darker streets,

as you prefer the punctual to anything like passion.

35. Sidedoor

Half-past autumn,
and the bricks can't keep their secrets anymore
for those going
outside in or elsewhere.

Regulars prefer it this way—

glancing backward from sidedoors,
accepting strange invitations of their familiars,
beyond excellent dangers, saying
"Thank you too much."

Then you become the closed gate,
encased by dark wood paneling.
Always hope among silhouettes, you think.

But once in, you are left slapping the wall blindly,
desperate for a light switch.

36. Lunch on a Steel Beam

Don't like the taste of this, don't like the touch of that, which gets passed over to you by gloved hand. Stuck thirty stories up, up to no good, no way. Up for anything you once said, you accept everything, surely long on conjecture or the wind to blow elsewhere. Enjoying the horizon with the rest of desolation's angels, ha!, grinding teeth like a real steel walker. From here you are everywhere and impossible. Ever too high enough, hung and strung, heart strummed by the brutalities of a February day, when you become absorbed by the skyline itself. You can't feel your legs or much less see them. And that is your best news for the day.

37. Poltroons and Gimcracks

In the name of diddly-squat,
in one delinquent second,

the Assistant Deputy of Whatever and So Forth
speaks of tenebrous vicissitudes

when even the pits require decorum
and only winds become imperial.

Oh, tense beauty waits impatiently in the wings
at the Command Performance Social Club,

mobilized for celebration
during these dissembling times.

In tribute to hourly rates,
in the land of the fifty-five-gallon drum,

the Chief Minister of External Portfolios
seems a perfectly normal nuisance.

Vacant, plaid-clad figures circle
around a behind-the-scenes map.

Scentless, home. Simply
one word away from ending a career

in a dark mull,
in the glint of the noonday gun.

38. Manholes

Your quaquaversal outlook
is a must being up, down, all around
the sewer, which always wins.

Near-dawn cold getting colder, steam
escaping from tooth-short mouths,
your headlight descending
gallantly, rung by rung,

bedeviled by consequences
of black water thickening
in the intestines of the city.

Soonest, you will wade
in isolation and spontaneity,
solitary as a spider.

39. Fanfare for a Cocktail

For John Dunn

Expedition of the eye swaying
casually halfway
through this stylish parquet room spread
before us and before the first
buckets of ice arrive. Soon say hello

to further stories of someone's ex,
or missing cat or your own high jinks
extraordinaire, in the swell name
of some other one's willingness.

The city sings the city's brilliance again
as sunset brings repentance
to those here herded high enough
to observe evening's first sparkles
at penthouse level. Cocksure,

you begin asking for a little something
on the rocks. Cold comfort and the threat
of sustenance, with a twist.
To the rescue, a great terrace view

requiring constant adjustment
and replenishment. The push
of the plush keeps one moving
continually, knowing nothing's
to be said without cocktail in hand.

Oh, the plenitudes and bloodlines,
the tweaking and ice leaking.
Much danger in a life
forgiven by too many precautions.

40. Cleaning the Statues

6 A.M. Hosing down the heroes
again and again. Ceremoniously
pushing broom and praise,

washing off the stains
of official explanation
without independent observation,

as we hatch a plot
to rid a famous concrete crotch
of pesky birds' nests.

Elegiac vortices, historical
trash, calls for "Speech, speech"
from the civic marble

close up, passionately meaningless,
long on puff, almost
flailing, failing indeed,

at another last chance for history to change.

Illinois Poetry Series

Laurence Lieberman, Editor

History Is Your Own Heartbeat
Michael S. Harper (1971)

The Foreclosure
Richard Emil Braun (1972)

The Scrawny Sonnets and Other
Narratives
Robert Bagg (1973)

The Creation Frame
Phyllis Thompson (1973)

To All Appearances: Poems New
and Selected
Josephine Miles (1974)

The Black Hawk Songs
Michael Borich (1975)

Nightmare Begins Responsibility
Michael S. Harper (1975)

The Wichita Poems
Michael Van Walleghen (1975)

Images of Kin: New and Selected
Poems
Michael S. Harper (1977)

Poems of the Two Worlds
Frederick Morgan (1977)

Cumberland Station
Dave Smith (1977)

Tracking
Virginia R. Terris (1977)

Riversongs
Michael Anania (1978)

On Earth as It Is
Dan Masterson (1978)

Coming to Terms
Josephine Miles (1979)

Death Mother and Other Poems
Frederick Morgan (1979)

Goshawk, Antelope
Dave Smith (1979)

Local Men
James Whitehead (1979)

Searching the Drowned Man
Sydney Lea (1980)

With Akhmatova at the Black
Gates
Stephen Berg (1981)

Dream Flights
Dave Smith (1981)

More Trouble with the Obvious
Michael Van Walleghen (1981)

The American Book of the Dead
Jim Barnes (1982)

The Floating Candles
Sydney Lea (1982)

Northbook
Frederick Morgan (1982)

Collected Poems, 1930–83
Josephine Miles (1983; reissue,
1999)

The River Painter
Emily Grosholz (1984)

Healing Song for the Inner Ear
Michael S. Harper (1984)

The Passion of the Right-Angled
Man
T. R. Hummer (1984)

Dear John, Dear Coltrane
Michael S. Harper (1985)

Poems from the Sangamon
John Knoepfle (1985)

In It
Stephen Berg (1986)

The Ghosts of Who We Were
Phyllis Thompson (1986)

Moon in a Mason Jar
Robert Wrigley (1986)

Lower-Class Heresy
T. R. Hummer (1987)

Poems: New and Selected
Frederick Morgan (1987)

Furnace Harbor: A Rhapsody of
the North Country
Philip D. Church (1988)

Bad Girl, with Hawk
Nance Van Winckel (1988)

Blue Tango
Michael Van Walleghen (1989)

Eden
Dennis Schmitz (1989)

Waiting for Poppa at the
Smithtown Diner
Peter Serchuk (1990)

Great Blue
Brendan Galvin (1990)

What My Father Believed
Robert Wrigley (1991)

Something Grazes Our Hair
S. J. Marks (1991)

Walking the Blind Dog
G. E. Murray (1992)

Chance Ransom
Kevin Stein (2000)

House of Poured-Out Waters
Jane Mead (2001)

The Silent Singer: New and
Selected Poems
Len Roberts (2001)

The Salt Hour
J. P. White (2001)

Guide to the Blue Tongue
Virgil Suárez (2002)

The House of Song
David Wagoner (2002)

X =
Stephen Berg (2002)

Arts of a Cold Sun
G. E. Murray (2003)

Barter
Ira Sadoff (2003)

National Poetry Series

Eroding Witness
Nathaniel Mackey (1985)
Selected by Michael S. Harper

Palladium
Alice Fulton (1986)
Selected by Mark Strand

Cities in Motion
Sylvia Moss (1987)
Selected by Derek Walcott

The Hand of God and a Few
Bright Flowers
William Olsen (1988)
Selected by David Wagoner

The Great Bird of Love
Paul Zimmer (1989)
Selected by William Stafford

Stubborn
Roland Flint (1990)
Selected by Dave Smith

The Surface
Laura Mullen (1991)
Selected by C. K. Williams

The Dig
Lynn Emanuel (1992)
Selected by Gerald Stern

My Alexandria
Mark Doty (1993)
Selected by Philip Levine

The High Road to Taos
Martin Edmunds (1994)
Selected by Donald Hall

Theater of Animals
Samn Stockwell (1995)
Selected by Louise Glück

The Broken World
Marcus Cafagña (1996)
Selected by Yusef Komunyakaa

Nine Skies
A. V. Christie (1997)
Selected by Sandra McPherson

Lost Wax
Heather Ramsdell (1998)
Selected by James Tate

So Often the Pitcher Goes to
Water until It Breaks
Rigoberto González (1999)
Selected by Ai

Renunciation
Corey Marks (2000)
Selected by Philip Levine

Manderley
Rebecca Wolff (2001)
Selected by Robert Pinsky

Theory of Devolution
David Groff (2002)
Selected by Mark Doty

Other Poetry Volumes

Local Men and *Domains*
James Whitehead (1987)

Her Soul beneath the Bone:
Women's Poetry on Breast Cancer
Edited by Leatrice Lifshitz (1988)

Days from a Dream Almanac
Dennis Tedlock (1990)

Working Classics: Poems on
Industrial Life
*Edited by Peter Oresick and
Nicholas Coles* (1990)

Hummers, Knucklers, and Slow
Curves: Contemporary Baseball
Poems
Edited by Don Johnson (1991)

The Double Reckoning of
Christopher Columbus
Barbara Helfgott Hyett (1992)

Selected Poems
Jean Garrigue (1992)

New and Selected Poems,
1962–92
Laurence Lieberman (1993)

The Dig and *Hotel Fiesta*
Lynn Emanuel (1994)

For a Living: The Poetry of Work
*Edited by Nicholas Coles and
Peter Oresick* (1995)

The Tracks We Leave: Poems on
Endangered Wildlife of North
America
Barbara Helfgott Hyett (1996)

Peasants Wake for Fellini's
Casanova and Other Poems
*Andrea Zanzotto; edited and
translated by John P. Welle and
Ruth Feldman; drawings by
Federico Fellini and Augusto
Murer* (1997)

Moon in a Mason Jar and *What
My Father Believed*
Robert Wrigley (1997)

The Wild Card: Selected Poems,
Early and Late
*Karl Shapiro; edited by Stanley
Kunitz and David Ignatow* (1998)

Turtle, Swan and *Bethlehem in
Broad Daylight*
Mark Doty (2000)

Illinois Voices: An Anthology of
Twentieth-Century Poetry
*Edited by Kevin Stein and
G. E. Murray* (2001)

On a Wing of the Sun
Jim Barnes (3-volume reissue,
2001)

Poems
*William Carlos Williams;
introduction by Virginia M.
Wright-Peterson* (2002)

The University of Illinois Press
is a founding member of the
Association of American University Presses.

Composed in 10/13 Galliard
with Nofret display
by Jim Proefrock
at the University of Illinois Press
Designed by Dennis Roberts
Manufactured by Cushing-Malloy, Inc.

University of Illinois Press
1325 South Oak Street
Champaign, IL 61820-6903
www.press.uillinois.edu